D1470289

What's it Like to

Be the Vet?

By: Marcy Blesy and Dr. Ed Blesy

## Introduction

So, you want to be the vet. Maybe you love animals. Maybe you like science and understanding how things work. But what is it *really* like to be the vet? What happens in the typical day of a veterinarian? What kinds of cases do doctors see? How do you take care of creatures that can't talk to you? What if things do not go well? How hard is it to tell owners that their dog or cat cannot get better? There are challenges with being a veterinarian that can create moments of both intense stress and joy. I am married to one of the veterinarians interviewed for this book, Dr. Ed Blesy. The stories I have heard over the last twenty years have been surprising, hilarious, sad, horrifying, and heartwarming. We want to share with you some of the stories from real vets in hopes that you get a flavor of the life of a vet—what it takes to be a vet and what you might see or do that perhaps you had not considered. To protect the privacy of the veterinarians interviewed in this book and their clients and patients, the names have been changed. However, the stories are all true. The names of the doctors that participated in this book are listed in the back. They are dedicated professionals to their clients and patients. Enjoy their stories.

## Why Did I Become a Vet?

This question is often asked of people who have chosen a particular profession. It is not a career that people just find themselves in one day. Most veterinarians attend eight years of school—four years at a university or college followed by four additional years at a veterinary school. That is a lot of money and time one must commit to being a veterinarian. Many vets spend years paying off the debt they acquired from going to college for so long. So, choosing this profession has to be a passion of some sort for most doctors.

Dr. Tom explains his decision to become a vet this way, "I always loved animals. I had all kinds of different pets including dogs, cats, pigeons, fish, quail, lizards, and even a tarantula." Having experience with animals as a child seems to be common among all of the doctors I interviewed. Dr. Jacob, who works with large animals (farm animals) as well as small animals (common household pets like dogs and cats) had two special animals that made a lasting impact on him as a child. "I had two calves, Chip and Dale. I wanted to raise them to be a team of oxen and then sell them to help me pay for college. One of them got pneumonia and died. I was very upset and determined then to become a vet so I could help sick animals." Dr. Amy also had many animals as a child. "My parents were breeders of champion German Shepherds, so I was playing with puppies since I was a baby. We also had sheep, horses, cats, and rabbits. I wanted to be a vet because I saw my parents' veterinarian helping our pets when they were injured or sick." Dr. Megan also grew up on a farm. "I spent a lot of time with my grandpa who would take care of any animal that needed help. I worked for a veterinarian in high school and decided that it was the career for me." Volunteering at a vet clinic also gave Dr. John an interest in being a vet. He did not grow up around a lot of animals—only cats. Growing up in the city of Chicago, he also did not have experience with farm animals. Instead, he worked at a vet clinic in high school "I thought I could make a decent living being a vet, and it was a well-respected career. I love nature and animals."

All of our doctors knew by high school that being a veterinarian might be the right career choice for them. You can never start too young thinking about your future. Don't worry, though, if you don't have it all figured out. Most people don't.

## Being the New Vet on the Job

After finishing eight years of college, you might think you would know everything you need to know to be the vet. *Wrong.* "When I first became a vet, one surprise was I had not learned much in vet school that helped me in day-to-day practice," said Dr. Amy. Dr. John agreed. "I didn't realize how unprepared I was coming out of vet school. Most of the education is in the real world and learned on the job." Dr. Henry said, "I was surprised how much there was still to learn. I had finished vet school and thought I knew almost everything. Then I learned I didn't and would always need to learn more and more so I could best treat my patients."

Dr. Brett was surprised by how hard the job was physically. It can also be a mentally taxing job when trying to figure out a tough case. When Dr. Mark started his first job as a vet, he had a difficult case that taught him the importance of asking for a good history of the animals being treated. "I had a case right out of vet school. Two out of ten cows were down in a field. They were still living but very sick. Everything pointed to a toxicity (poisoning), so I questioned the owners about possible exposure to toxins. They knew nothing. I searched the ten acres for poisonous plants and saw nothing. I treated them symptomatically (the signs of illness they were showing) but got a call the next day that they had died and two more were sick. I did a necropsy (cut the animal open after it died to look for signs as to the cause of death) and found that the rumens (the largest part of a cow's four chamber stomach) had Yew bush pine needles in them. I asked the owners about how they could have Yew bush needles in their stomachs when no Yews were in the field. They informed me that they had trimmed bushes around the house and threw the trimmings in the field. They were eaten completely, so no evidence."

The case taught Dr. Mark the importance of asking the owners lots of questions when trying to solve a tricky case.

There are other "hats" that vets have to wear besides being the doctor. One of those "hats" Dr. Jacob learned about after he came out of vet school and started working. "I quickly learned that you need a lot of business sense in veterinary work that you don't always learn in vet school. I have to be a business man, too." There's more to being a vet than just making an animal feel better.

Several vets discovered the importance of working with owners when on the job. "I was surprised how you can get so close and emotionally attached to families and their pets," said Dr. Tom. Dr. Megan realized something similar. "I didn't realize until I started working just how much I had to work with people. Most all of the animals I work on have a person at the other end of the leash or lead rope or holding the carrier. And I need to work with them to find out what has been going on with the animal to be able to help them." This part of the job can be challenging but also positive. "I was surprised I enjoyed knowing the people because I had always been an *animal person* and quite shy," said Dr. Amy. "I had to take care of the person *holding* the senior kitty as well as the pet."

No one knows everything at the start of a new career. Job experience is often the best educator. New vets take everything they have learned in school and apply it to real life situations which teaches them things they never knew they needed to know.

## Typical Day

The doctors were asked to describe their typical work day. Of course, the days vary because every clinic is unique as is every doctor. However, Dr. John answered the question easily. "There is no typical day." Dr. Jacob agreed. "I do large and small animal medicine. Every day is different. You don't know what to expect."

However, most doctors find a balance between seeing appointments and doing surgeries. "Three days a week I see appointments all day, a mix of well visits for vaccinations (to help animals stay healthy) and sick pets. One day I spend the morning doing surgery and the afternoon seeing appointments. Occasionally, I will have a day where I do farm calls for horses, cattle, pigs, or goats, or a house call (checking a sick animal at home)," said Dr. Megan. "I see morning appointments and then surgeries until lunch," said Dr. Tom. "Appointments are seen in the afternoon and early evening. I take phone messages throughout the day." Dr. Henry also makes time to be there for his patients who are not in his office. "In between appointments or during breaks, I make phone calls about test results or answer questions from concerned pet parents. I also finish any records that I couldn't earlier." (Records include information about the pet and the doctor's recommendations for treatment.)

Dr. John has time for lunch built into his schedule, but it doesn't always happen. "I hope to have a lunch, but sometimes emergencies arise." "A typical day can often have surprises. Sometimes something I haven't seen before comes in, but I learned from these challenging cases," said Dr. Amy. "Occasionally, I have to do surgery like suturing a laceration or treating a bite wound. Sometimes pets have been hit by cars. That is often challenging," she said.

There are veterinarians who treat farm (large) animals and household (small) animals. However, some doctors progress in their career with more specialized training. For example, some doctors get extra training to be an animal ophthalmologist to treat eye problems or an orthopedic surgeon to treat bone injuries. Dr. Brett said his days are much different now from his days as a small animal doctor. "I always enjoyed teaching and now take my show on the road. I continue to provide continuing education lectures and educate veterinarians on how to help animals with new therapies, instead of the clients."

Confused yet? There is no one answer as to what a veterinarian does every day because it changes every day. There is no typical day. However, all vets have the same goal—to keep your animals healthy and safe or free from pain—whatever way they can. Wouldn't life be boring if every day was exactly the same? Boredom is *not* an adjective

that describes the veterinary profession.

**Let's See Some Cases.**

## Funny Cases

For this section I asked the veterinarians to describe some of the funny cases or pets they have seen during their careers. With all the tough cases that can arise in a typical week, sometimes an amusing case lessens the stress, especially when all turns out well.


## Some problems aren't problems at all.

*"An elderly owner brought a toy poodle dog in for limping problems. It simply had two long toenails that were criss-crossed. Problem solved!"*   Dr. Brett


## Some problems are smelly and can be laughed about *after the fact.*

*"I once had an anal gland squirt in my face. And a vet tech (veterinarian's assistant) was putting a hot pack on a giant abscess*

*(pus filled sore) when it ruptured all over spilling out smelly, nasty pus." Dr. John*

**Sometimes saving an animal can involve a little bit of luck.**

*"I had a big German Shepard with a large fishing lure lodged deep in his throat. As I put my gloved finger deep in his throat to visualize, the dog tried to bite me. As I quickly retracted my finger out of his throat, the hook dug into my glove, quickly and miraculously removing the fishing lure. Sure...I meant to do that!" Dr. Tom*

**You said the dog's head is *where?***

*"I've had several pets come in because they had their heads caught in a jar or a funnel. One was a young tomcat that had his head stuck in a mayonnaise jar that he had licked totally clean. But then his paws were too greasy to get the jar off his head, so he looked like a*

*little spaceman. Once I saw a stray German Shepherd puppy that the owners found with his head stuck in a peanut butter jar. After the jar came off his head, the owners kept him and named him* Jar. *I always enjoyed seeing* Jar *because he turned out to be a great dog after his humble beginnings." Dr. Amy*

*"I had a dog come in who had his head stuck inside a wheel. We had to sedate him (put him to sleep for a short time) and make his fur all greasy so we could get him out of it!" Dr. Megan*

**When you are friends or family with a veterinarian, you must always be alert.**

*"I was a vet at a zoo. There was a bacterial disease outbreak in the reptile house, and I was treating them. I went out late on a Saturday evening after office hours to the zoo. I treated some snakes and took one back to the clinic that had died so I could perform a necropsy to see why the animal had died. Being late on a Saturday, I*

decided to do the necropsy the next day and took the snake coiled in a plastic bag and put it in my refrigerator at home. I forgot to tell my wife what was in the refrigerator. About two hours later, I heard a blood curdling scream from the kitchen. I immediately realized that she had gone into the refrigerator, and I was in big trouble." Dr. Mark

"My wife used to go on emergency calls with me when we were first married. I had to sedate a dog to do emergency surgery. She had never seen an animal under sedation, and she thought I had killed the dog. Luckily, she has more faith in me now!" Dr. John

## Sad Cases

Unfortunately, part of being a vet is working with animals that suffer or are too sick to fix. In order to fully understand the job of being a veterinarian, it is important to learn about the harsh reality of losing an animal. Doctors share their stories below.

*"I have had clients lose pets in fires. Many times the owners have lost everything they own, AND their beloved pet."* Dr. Brett

*"When people can't pay for their dog when it is severely injured or ill, it is always sad. Also, it is tough if someone is walking a dog and it is attacked or gets run over by a car. I once had a woman run over her own dog with a lawnmower. It did not die. We stabilized it and sent the dog to an emergency clinic and saved it. If the owner did not have money, the dog may have been euthanized (life of the pet ended with compassion)."* Dr. John

*"A cat that I declawed (removed the front claws), died in recovery after surgery. It was the beloved cat owned by a little boy with Cystic Fibrosis."* Dr. Tom

*"I had a client who owned a bookstore, and her dog went to work at the bookstore with her. He was also a therapy dog. He got a fungal infection that we worked really hard to cure. He did well for a while. But then the infection came back in his heart, and we couldn't save him."* Dr Megan

*"It's heartbreaking to see animals struggle. We once had a cat who was so full of maggots that we could hear the maggots eating the flesh of the cat."* Dr. John

This part of the job is difficult. However, veterinarians must be ready to handle any situation that arises. Being compassionate to their clients, patients, and themselves is important.

## More Memorable Cases

I wanted to give the doctors a chance to tell us about some of the more memorable cases in their careers. It is sometimes a pet that a vet has treated for years that a doctor remembers. Other times it is an unusual case or unusual owner that is difficult to forget.

*"I once treated a rabbit with a bungee cord hook wrapped around its cheek bone. After a little sedation, we had it out like nothing happened."* Dr. Brett

*"I had a Golden Retriever who had its front leg stuck in the head of a combine out in the middle of 200 acres of corn. It was lodged above her elbow. I had to amputate (cut off) the leg out in the field followed by more surgery at the clinic to clean things up. I felt like I was in a battlefield."* Dr. Tom

"I sutured up (sewed) a dog after its nose got chopped off by a brush chopper along the road. I also removed a spleen tumor from a dog. The tumor was larger than a basketball. The dog lived for years. Another time, a dog came in that was having sneezing fits and rubbing its face. I was able to see just a little bit of green inside the nose. I used a hemostat and reached in to pull out a piece of grass. It was four inches long!" Dr. John


"A dog was run over by its owner and had a broken leg. The owner was a rough, gruff, old farmer. I told him that I could fix the leg and his dog would be fine. It would cost X dollars. He was surprised by the cost and said that he had never spent that much money on a dog. He then walked over to me and got within a foot of my face. He said if he ever heard at the coffee shop from his friends in the future what he paid to treat the dog, I'd be in trouble. The dog did fine, and I kept my mouth shut as I always did!" Dr. Mark

*"Recently I saw a three-year-old Basset Hound named Marshall. He was coughing. The family's last Basset died sadly from cancer, so I felt extra pressure to help Marshall. So, what I thought was a simple kennel cough or infectious bronchitis was actually fungal pneumonia. His lungs were white on an X-ray instead of black like normal because he was full of infection. I finally got the diagnosis by doing a urine test for blastomycosis. He must have sniffed up some dirt with the fungus. Marshall started on the medication for the fungal infection. At first, he got worse because the fungal organisms were dying off causing an allergic reaction. I treated Marshall with Prednisone, and that night he was doing much better. I often pray for my client and patients and for wisdom to diagnose and determine the right treatment plans."   Dr. Amy*

## Naughty Pets

Dogs and cats often act like toddlers. They like to put things into their mouths that do not belong there. Our vets have lots of cautionary examples of animals that needed veterinary treatment after eating things that did not belong in their bodies.

"What haven't I seen dogs eat?" said Dr. John. Dogs do not always make the most logical choices. Dr. Henry has seen dogs eat many odd things such as balls, leashes, boxing glove wraps, bones, and human hair. "One dog ate his doggie door—metal and all," said Dr. Amy. "Our technician's dog ate a squeaker from his Christmas present. It floated around in his stomach for two months. It got stuck in his intestine and had to be removed surgically," she said.

Dr. Mark has a client with a pet who favored one very unique item. "A good client brought in a young dog with an intestinal obstruction (something stuck). I performed surgery and removed a pair of women's underwear. This happened four more times over the life of the dog—always women's underwear. When we euthanized the dog for severe arthritis in his later years, I was asked to perform a necropsy for a breed study that they were doing. Guess what the dog had in his stomach? Yup—women's underwear." Dr. Brett's patient kept eating cloth napkins. "Every few months the dog would come in. Usually the problem was solved by making the dog vomit."

Dr. Jacob found the stomachs of two dogs in a very unique shape. They had ingested a very strong glue called Gorilla Glue. "After opening them up, I found the glue was in the shape of their stomachs." Other items Dr. Jacob has seen ingested by his patients include peach pits, super hero figures, ornaments, and bouncy balls. Dr. Megan's patients have eaten owner's medications, *lots* of chocolate, eyeglasses, coins, batteries, garbage, socks, rugs, baby pacifiers, and rat poison.

Even veterinarian's *own* dogs have been naughty. Dr. John's dog ate a box of crayons. Needless to say, his dog had *very* colorful poop. Dr. Amy's dog ate a whole bottle of baby oil. "Thank goodness it wasn't toxic. But it oozed out for several days, and the odor was unbelievable!"

Some things that dogs eat are simply amusing and not harmful. However, many things can get stuck inside an animal, or even be toxic, like certain pennies that may have zinc, as Dr. Amy told me. Be very careful to watch you dog, especially when you have a puppy. Those little critters have minds of their own! And sometimes they are up to no good!

"Cats are a lot more picky about what they eat," said Dr. Megan. Still, that doesn't stop them from causing trouble and earning a trip to see the vet. Some of the more common items munched on by cats are fish hooks, strings, floss, human hair, yarn, and cat toys.

"Cats have a hard time spitting things out because the rasps on their tongue point to their throat, so when they get a string or piece of thread caught in their mouth, it's very hard for them to spit it out," said Dr. Amy. "We have taken a lot of strings and threads out of cats because they can't pass the intestine. I once removed a six foot long piece of curling ribbon the cat had eaten from a balloon. The owner found the helium balloon with just a little piece of ribbon left on it, and her cat was vomiting. Easy diagnosis, tough surgery! I had to make six different incisions in the stomach and intestine to get the ribbon out, but the kitty did great and lived a long life," she said.

Many of the vets talked about the amount of hair bands they have seen cats eat. "One time, someone called because their cat was throwing up. We took an X-ray and his tummy looked funny inside," said Dr. Henry. "We did a second test and saw all these circles that looked like rubber bands. The kitty had surgery, and I removed 43 hair bands! The cat's owners didn't even know how many years this had been happening. After surgery, my patient was as good as new!"

Just as with dogs, cats can be seriously hurt when eating things that are not good for them. In addition to things getting stuck, they can also burn their mouths chewing on cords or get sick from eating things like potpourri or certain plants, Dr. John told me. Watch those cats that live in your home. They are sneaky!

**Owners**

Helping to heal a sick pet cannot happen without the help of the owner of the pet. Since dogs, cats, and farm animals cannot talk, the veterinarians rely upon their owners to communicate the problems the animal has been having. Dealing with owners is both a wonderful *and* challenging part of the job.

"I like getting to know different people and the different ways they live and their perspective on different things," said Dr. Jacob. "I love people, so working with them every day to help keep their pet healthy is very rewarding. Owners who bring in a sick pet are often worried, but if they can leave with their pet feeling better and feeling better themselves, then I know I am doing my job. It's a good feeling for me as the doctor," said Dr. Henry. Pets are more than *just pets* to their owners. "I just feel really honored that people entrust me with their pet's care. I know a lot of the clients feel like their pets are their children," said Dr. Amy.

However, not all interactions with owners go smoothly. "There are always some people that you cannot please no matter what you do, but they are fortunately rare," said Dr. Megan. "It is most challenging when the owners are worried. I can help make a lot of people feel better if I explain things to them, but sometimes clients are so worried that they can't listen very well. Then they can also be a little unkind to me or my team because they aren't thinking clearly," said Dr. Henry. "Sometimes you can't do anything for an animal, and that's frustrating to the doctor and the owners," said Dr. John.

Many of the vets mentioned that money issues can be a source of conflict between the doctor and the owners. "The biggest challenge is always money. There are many times I could do a lot more for the pet, but the owner cannot afford the best treatment. There are also a small number of people who think that I work on animals for free because I love them," said Dr. Megan.

To ensure the best treatment for an animal's health, the owner and doctor need to communicate openly with each other. If both parties listen to each other and share their concerns, the animal will benefit.

## Other Challenges on the Job

If you are thinking about becoming a veterinarian, you need to know the positives *and* negatives to have a fuller picture about the job. We will discuss the frustrations of the job first.

Some veterinarians do not live near 24-hour emergency vet clinics. They often take emergency calls after hours to be available for their clients. Having to be on call was mentioned by a couple of these vets as a challenge. The hours and stress of the job is a reality in this profession.

"I think losing a patient is always hard but I think its hardest when the problem was preventable or when the owners wait too long to let them go, and it seems that they have been suffering for a long time," said Dr. Amy. Also, "having a financial threshold that prevents you from giving proper treatment is hard," said Dr. Jacob." "I don't like when money gets in the way of treating pets. But it is a reality," said Dr. Tom.

Being a veterinarian is a huge time commitment. The job often *comes home* with the doctors. They think about their clients. They make calls from home. They finish records. They are on call for their patients. It is sometimes hard to find time to close their minds off from their jobs, and everyone needs a break sometimes. However, dedicated vets would not continue in their jobs if there weren't many positive things that balance the challenges.

## Joys on the Job

"Being a veterinarian is mostly a well-respected profession," said Dr. John. "I like helping animals and people." This is kind of a requirement for the job of being a vet—wanting to help pet owners and their animals.

Dr. Tom also enjoys meeting new people. "Knowing people from all walks of life and being their friend is great," he said. Also, variety makes things enjoyable for Drs. Megan and Jacob. "I like that every day is different—different animals, different illnesses, and at my clinic I may work inside or outside on anything from a newborn kitten or puppy to a draft horse," said Dr. Megan. "Variety in the job is nice," said Dr. Jacob.

"My favorite thing is seeing puppies and kittens. I like teaching my clients how to take the best care of their pets so they will hopefully live a long, healthy life," said Dr. Amy.

Every job has positives and negatives. Consider it all when choosing your career. Hopefully, whatever you choose to do with your life, the joys will outweigh the challenges.

**So, You Want to Be the Vet: Advice**

Our veterinarians have lots of advice for you if you are considering a career as a veterinarian. Think about these things as you form your ideas about your future.

1. Get good grades.

2. Study hard.

3. Be involved in organizations.

4. Build your leadership skills.

5. Volunteer or get a job at a veterinary clinic while you are younger.

6. Volunteer at a shelter.

7. Be compassionate towards animals and people.

8. Take business and communication classes in high school and college.

9. Understand the financial commitment of veterinary school.

10. Apply for every scholarship you think you have a chance at.

11. Learn everything you can. Read books about the profession.

12. Visit the American Veterinary Medical Association website (AVMA).

"Being a veterinarian is not a job but a way of life," said Dr. Brett. Dr. John agreed. "It is a career of passion," he said.

"If becoming a veterinarian is your passion in life, then you can absolutely do it! There is a lot you can do with a veterinary degree in addition to being a small animal veterinarian. For example, you could do research into cures for people and animals," said Dr. Amy.

Still want to be a veterinarian? There are animals of all shapes and sizes and kinds waiting for your loving care to make their lives better. Find a vet. Talk to him or her. Learn all that you can. You *will* be making a difference in the world.

\*\*\*\*\*\*\*\*\*\*\*\*\*\*\*\*\*\*\*\*\*\*\*\*\*\*\*\*\*\*\*\*\*\*\*\*\*\*\*\*\*\*\*\*\*\*\*\*\*\*\*\*\*\*\*\*\*\*\*\*\*\*\*\*

**Fun Facts:**

## Common Dog Names:

Leo, Bear, Bella, Max, Buddy, Lexie, Brizzo (Bryant and Rizzo combined from the Chicago Cubs), Lucky, Charlie, Duke, Daisy, Molly, Sam, Fluffy, Jake, Sophie, Lady, Riley, Cooper

## Common Cat Names:

Tiger, Tigger, Gracie, Tabby, Midnight, Ally, Mabel, Mia, Sassy, Fluffy, Oreo, Spots, Kitty, Tom, Tux, Socks, Louie, Felix, Shadow

## Unique Animals Our Vets Have Treated:

Think that vets only treat dogs and cats? Think again!

Here is a list of other animals our vets have seen:


hedgehog, great horned owl, 60 pound tortoise named Solomon, macaw, camel, snake, rabbit, birds, alligator, seal (at the zoo), homing pigeons, ostriches, turkey vulture, snapping turtle, lizards, rats, bison, ducks, deer, raccoon, pot belly pigs, llamas, alpacas, gerbils, guinea pigs, bearded dragons, zebras

\*\*\*\*\*\*\*\*\*\*\*\*\*\*\*\*\*\*\*\*\*\*\*\*\*\*\*\*\*\*\*\*\*\*\*\*\*\*\*\*\*\*\*\*\*\*\*\*\*\*\*\*\*\*\*\*\*\*\*\*

Thank you very much to the wonderful, caring, dedicated veterinarians who have taken the time out of their busy schedules to answer questions for this book. Their clients and patients are very lucky to have them.

Dr. Edmund Blesy

Dr. Janelle Bols

Dr. Todd Duffy

Dr. David Gonsky

Dr. Terrance O'Brien

Dr. Craig Stevenson

Dr. Christy Stockdale

Dr. Kevin Zollars

**Other Be the Vet books:**

*Be the Vet:*

Do you like dogs and cats?

Have you ever thought about being a veterinarian?

Place yourself as the narrator in seven unique stories about dogs and cats. When a medical emergency or illness impacts the pet, you will have the opportunity to diagnose the problem and suggest treatment. Following each story is the treatment plan offered by Dr. Ed Blesy, a 20 year practicing veterinarian. You will learn veterinary terms and diagnoses while being entertained with fun, interesting stories.

This is the first book in the BE THE VET series.

For ages 9-12

*Be the Vet, Volume 2*

**Reviews for *Be the Vet:***

"Be the Vet - 7 Dog and Cat Stories - Test Your Veterinary Knowledge" is an entertaining teaching tool for pet lovers. Highly recommended.

---Midwest Book Review, June 2014

Seasoned veterinarian Dr. Ed Blesy and his wife Marcy collaborate in "Be the Vet." The book is a unique concept made up of heart- touching stories, creative diagnostic assignments for readers ages 9 - 13, with informative recommended treatment plans.


---From an Amazon Top 500  Reviewer

**Other Children's Books by Marcy Blesy:**

*Evie and the Volunteers Series*

*Join ten-year-old Evie and her friends as they volunteer all over town meeting lots of cool people and getting into just a little bit of trouble. There is no place left untouched by their presence, and what they get from the people they meet is greater than any amount of money.*

*Book 1   Animal Shelter*

*Book 2   Nursing Home*

*Book 3   After-School Program*

*Book 4   Food Pantry*

*Book 5:   Public Library*

*Book 6:   Hospital*

*Book 7:   Military Care Packages*

*Dax and the Destroyers:* (a new *Evie and the Volunteers spin-off)*

### Book 1:  House Flip

*Twelve-year-old Dax spends the summer with his Grandma. When a new family moves into the run-down house across the street, Dax finds a fast friend in their son Harrison. Not to be outdone by his friends, Evie and the Volunteers, and all of their good deeds, Dax finds himself immersed in the business of house flipping as well as Harrison's family drama. But don't expect things to go smoothly when Evie and her friends get word of this new volunteer project. Everyone has an opinion about flipping this house.*

### Book 2:  Park Restoration

### *Am I Like My Daddy?*

Join seven-year-old Grace on her journey through coping with the loss of her father while learning about the different ways that people grieve the loss of a loved one. In the process of learning about who her father was through the eyes of others, she learns about who she is today because of her father's personality and love. *Am I Like My Daddy?* is a book designed to help children who are coping with the loss of a loved one. Children are encouraged to express through journaling what may be so difficult to express through everyday conversation. *Am I Like My Daddy?* teaches about loss through reflection.

*Am I Like My Daddy?* is an important book in the children's grief genre. Many books in this genre deal with the time immediately after a loved one dies. This book focuses on years after the death, when a maturing child is reprocessing his or her grief. New questions arise in the child's need to fill in those memory gaps.